MY
ROSARY
NOVENA

By

REV. LAWRENCE G. LOVASIK, S.V.D.
Divine Word Missionary

•

**With the addition of
the New Luminous Mysteries
of Pope John Paul II**

CATHOLIC BOOK PUBLISHING CORP.
New Jersey

NIHIL OBSTAT: Sr. M. Kathleen Flanagan, S.C., Ph.D.
Censor Librorum

IMPRIMATUR: ✠ Frank J. Rodimer, J.C.D.
Bishop of Paterson

(T-20)

ISBN 978-0-89942-021-9

MEDITATION

THE Rosary is a favorite means of devotion to the Blessed Virgin Mary, recommended by the Popes over many centuries. It consists of various elements:

a) *Contemplation,* in union with Mary, of a series of Mysteries of Salvation, distributed into four cycles. These Mysteries express (1) the joy of the Messianic times, (2) events from Christ's Public Ministry (called Mysteries of Light or Luminous Mysteries*), (3) the suffering of Christ, and (4) the glory of the Risen Lord which fills the Church. This contemplation by its very nature encourages practical reflection and provides norms for living.

---

* Suggested by Pope John Paul II in his Apostolic Letter of Oct. 16, 2002, entitled *The Rosary of the Virgin Mary.*

b) *The Lord's Prayer*, which by reason of its immense value is at the basis of Christian prayer and ennobles that prayer in its various expressions.

c) The litany-like succession of the *Hail Mary*, which is made up of the Angel's greeting to the Virgin (Lk 1:28) and of Elizabeth's greeting (Lk 1:42), followed by the Church's own prayer. The continued series of Hail Marys is the special characteristic of the Rosary, and their number (200) is divided into decades attached to the individual Mysteries.

d) The doxology *Glory be to the Father* concludes the prayer with the glorifying of God Who is One and Three, from Whom, through Whom, and in Whom all things have their being (Rom 11:36).

In her sixth and last apparition at Fatima, October 13, 1917, the Blessed Virgin insisted on the recitation of the Rosary as a powerful means for the conversion of Russia and for peace in the world. When Lucy asked, "Who are you and what do you want?" Our Lady replied: "I am the Lady of the Rosary, and I have come to warn the faithful to amend their lives and ask pardon for their sins. They must not continue to offend our Lord Who is already so deeply offended. They must say the Rosary."

Through the prayer of the Rosary untold blessings have been showered down upon all humankind throughout the ages. Through the Rosary today as in past times of peril that have threatened civilization, Mary has again come to save all humankind from the evils that overwhelm us.

But the Rosary is especially most helpful in bringing back home life to its full splendor, by raising the family to a higher family circle where God is Father and Mary is Mother and we are all children of God. The Family Rosary is a practical way to strengthen the unity of family life.

THE WORD OF GOD

"Who is she that comes forth like the morning rising, as beautiful as the moon, as bright as the sun, as awe-inspiring as an army in battle array?"   —Song 6:10

"You are as beautiful as Tirzah [early capital of Northern Israel], as comely as Jerusalem, as awe-inspiring as an army in battle array."   —Song 6:4

"Listen to me, my faithful children: blossom like roses planted near a stream of water; send out your fragrance like incense, and break forth in blossoms like the lily. Scatter your fragrance and sing a hymn of praise; bless the Lord for all His works."   —Sir 39:13-14

NOVENA PRAYERS

Novena Prayer

M Y dearest Mother Mary, behold me, your child, in prayer at your feet. Accept this Holy Rosary, which I offer you in accordance with your requests at Fatima, as a proof of my tender love for you, for the intentions of the Sacred Heart of Jesus, in atonement for the offenses committed against your Immaculate Heart, and for this special favor which I earnestly request in my Rosary Novena: *(Mention your request).*

I beg you to present my petition to your Divine Son. If you will pray for me, I cannot be refused. I know, dearest Mother, that you want me to seek God's holy Will concerning my request. If what I ask for should not be granted, pray that I may receive that which will be of greater benefit to my soul.

I offer you this spiritual "Bouquet of Roses" because I love you. I put all my confidence in you, since your prayers before God are most powerful. For the greater glory of God and for the sake of Jesus, your loving Son, hear and grant my prayer. Sweet Heart of Mary, be my salvation.

THE HOLY ROSARY

ON the Cross: In the Name of the Father, etc. I believe in God, the Father Almighty, Creator of heaven and earth, and in Jesus Christ, His only Son, our Lord, Who was conceived by the Holy Spirit, born of the Virgin Mary, suffered under Pontius Pilate, was crucified, died and was buried; He descended into hell; on the third day He rose again from the dead; He ascended into heaven, and is seated at the right hand of God the Father Almighty; from there He will come to judge the living and the dead. I believe in the Holy Spirit, the Holy Catholic Church, the Communion of Saints, the forgiveness of sins, the resurrection of the body, and life everlasting. Amen.

On the first large bead: Our Father, etc.

On the next three beads: For an increase of faith, hope, and charity. Hail Mary, etc. (*3 times*).

Glory be to the Father, etc.

Fatima prayer (after each decade): "O my Jesus, forgive us our sins, save us from the fire of hell, take all souls to heaven, and help especially those most in need of Your mercy."

FIRST AND FIFTH DAY

1st Joyful Mystery

The Annunciation

Our Father . . .

JESUS, at the Annunciation God proposes the Mystery of Your Incarnation which will be fulfilled in the Blessed Virgin when she shall have given her free consent. Through the Angel Gabriel You invite her to become Your Mother. It seems as though You await the response of the humanity to which You wish to unite Yourself.

Full of faith, Mary gives her reply: "I am the servant of the Lord. Let it be done to me as you say." At this moment You, the Divine Word, the Second Person of the Holy Trinity, take flesh of the Virgin Mary and become Man, for the Angel said to her, "The Holy Spirit will come upon you and the power of the Most High will overshadow you; hence, the holy offspring to be born will be called Son of God."

This is the greatest event in the history of the world, for the salvation of human beings depends upon it. I thank You for having loved me so much as to become Man to save my soul. I thank You for having chosen the Virgin Mary as Your Mother. This Mystery has earned for her the most glorious of her titles, that of Mother of God, which makes her all-powerful with You, her Divine Son. Through Your Mother's intercession grant me the grace to save my soul.

Hail Mary. *(Ten times)*

Glory be to the Father . . .

"O my Jesus, forgive us our sins, save us from the fire of hell, take all souls to heaven, and help especially those most in need of Your mercy."

2nd Joyful Mystery

The Visitation

JESUS, in God's design the Visitation is the occasion when You reveal the fact of Your Incarnation and Your Mother's role as the dispenser of all graces. You work Your first miracle in Mary's womb by stirring the unborn John and making Elizabeth conscious of Your presence. You brought grace upon the earth and Your love made You bestow it at once through Your loving Mother. John the Baptist receives its first gift because his task is so closely connected with Your Person.

In this Mystery You wish to show us that Your Mother is the instrument and means by which You impart to us Your graces. I believe that all graces have their source in You, the Head of the Mystical Body, the Church. But these graces reach us, the members, through Mary, as if she were the neck of that Body. Where Mary is, there the springs of heavenly blessings flow more freely and more richly, because she bears in herself You, the Source of all grace. It is Your Will that she impart this grace to others. I thank You for making Your Mother the Mediatrix of All Graces.

3rd Joyful Mystery

The Birth of Our Lord

JESUS, with Mary and Joseph I kneel down in devout worship as I gaze upon You lying in Your crib. You wish to enter the world as a Child in order to prove Yourself to be true Man, for Your weeping and Your need for rest and nourishment are just so many proofs of Your true human nature. You become Human that we may be able to see You, listen to You, imitate You, and unite ourselves to You. Even though You are God, You are now able to suffer for us, atone for our sins, and merit graces for our souls. It is through the flesh that human beings turn away from God; it is in taking on the flesh that God delivers them.

But You become Man also that we may become like God. In exchange for the Humanity which You take from us, you wish to make us share in Your Divinity by sanctifying grace, that You may take complete possession of us.

May the Mystery of Your birth bring me the grace to be born again spiritually and live a new Divine life, more free from sin and from all attachment to myself and creatures—a life for God alone. As it was Mary's joy to form You in her own body, may her joy now be to form You in my soul.

4th Joyful Mystery

The Presentation in the Temple

 JESUS, by the union of Your Human Nature with the second Person of the Blessed Trinity You were consecrated to God. But this ceremony of presentation is Your first external consecration to Your priestly mission. As the Anointed of the Lord, the Long-Desired of Nations, You are brought for the first time into Your Temple, into Your Father's house.

In Your Mother's arms You offer Yourself to Your heavenly Father to be the Victim of our Redemption, as in future years You will continue to offer Yourself daily at Mass in the hands of numberless priests. No one can hear the words You utter while offering Yourself, but the secret thoughts of Your Sacred Heart are expressed by the lips of Your Blessed Mother as she offers You for the salvation of the world.

The aged Simeon, enlightened by the Holy Spirit, recognizes You as the Messiah. Joyfully he takes You in his arms and proclaims You to be "a revealing Light to the Gentiles."

You humbly and fervently offer Yourself to the Father by the hands of the ancient priesthood. Never has a greater offering been made to God in this Temple. The Most Holy Trinity and all heaven look down on it with delight.

5th Joyful Mystery

The Finding in the Temple

JESUS, I see You as a Boy of twelve in the Temple, standing in the midst of teachers who are amazed at Your wisdom and charmed by Your personality. It is here that Mary and Joseph find You after having sought You with sorrow for three days.

This Mystery reveals to me Your devoted love and tender reverence for Your Father. God alone is in Your heart, and nothing but His Will rules there; every other claim has to be silent before it.

You appear in the Temple to show that You must be about Your Father's work. Although You have a Mother and owe her loving obedience, You also have a Father Who is greater, and whose Will and command must be given first place. That Will and command is the promotion of His honor and the salvation of souls, which is Your life-work.

Let the glory of God and the salvation of souls, especially my own, be my only real concern in life. I wish to be attached to God alone by love as You always were, and to do His Holy Will in all things. May I put out of my heart desires for worldly things, and give God the first right to all that I have, especially to my love.

SECOND AND SIXTH DAY
1st Luminous Mystery
The Baptism of Jesus in the Jordan

JESUS, John the Baptist was Your forerunner to prepare the way for You. John exhorted the people to turn away from sin and be baptized, for the Kingdom of God was coming. He also told them that You were much greater than he was and would soon come and baptize them with the Holy Spirit and with fire. Thus, he prepared the way for Your saving mission.

One day, You appeared before John at the Jordan River and asked him to baptize You to set a good example for all. After Your baptism, the heavens were opened and the Holy Spirit descended upon You in bodily shape, like a dove. Then a voice from heaven said: "You are My Son, the Beloved; My favor rests on You."

Lord, the Holy Spirit descended not to make You holy, but, according to the Old Testament tradition, to anoint You for Your future mission. This Spirit was promised to the Messianic King of David's line, and God's Suffering Servant, by the Prophet Isaiah. The voice from heaven proclaimed You to be the Messiah-King, the Beloved, the only Son, spoken of by the

Prophet Isaiah. Your work was to be the sacrifice of the Cross, which You later called Your "baptism."

Jesus, I wish to take Your Father's advice to the disciples at Your Transfiguration and listen to You, not only when I read Your Gospel and study Your doctrine and example but also when You speak to me by Your grace and inspirations. Give me the grace to be constant in my obedience and to keep my Baptismal Promises so that I may make progress toward holiness.

2nd Luminous Mystery

Christ's Self-Manifestation at the Wedding in Cana

MARY, at the very beginning of Your Son's Public Ministry you went with Jesus and His disciples to a wedding of a friend in Cana of Galilee. At one point, the servants discovered that there was not enough wine for all the guests.

When this was brought to your attention, you went to Jesus and said simply, "They have no wine." Jesus said, "Dear Woman [which was a term of endearment], how does that concern Me? My hour has not yet come." Yet you, as the first believer in Jesus, knew that He would do something to help the situation. So you told the servants, "Do whatever He tells you."

Jesus had the servants fill six stone jars with water. Then He said, "Draw some water out and take it to the chief steward." What they drew out was no longer water but delicious wine. When the steward tasted it, he said to the bridegroom, "People generally serve the best wine first, and keep the cheaper kind till the guests have had enough to drink; but you have kept the best wine till now."

This was a sign of the wonderful power Jesus had, and which He used to help others. And His disciples also came to believe in Him.

In response to your innocent request and because of your ready obedience to whatever He decided, Jesus worked a miracle and manifested Himself. The wine points to the Messianic nature of Christ's mission, for wine represents His wisdom and teaching.

Mary, in this Mystery you showed yourself in your exalted character of Advocate. Jesus rewarded your confidence and resignation by working His first miracle at your request. In this I see God's plan that in your Son's Kingdom all graces go through your hand and heart.

Teach me to seek all things through you, O Mary, for your intercession is most powerful, and Christ can refuse you nothing. Help me to imitate your zeal in assisting my neighbor in his need and let me always do whatever Jesus tells me.

3rd Luminous Mystery

Christ's Proclamation of the Kingdom of God

JESUS, You began Your mission by proclaiming the Gospel of God and saying, "The time of fulfillment has arrived, and the Kingdom of God is close at hand. Repent, and believe in the Gospel." With Your call to forgiveness, You inaugurated the ministry of mercy, which You would continue to exercise until the end of the world, particularly through the Sacrament of Reconciliation.

Then in the Sermon on the Mount, You gave the qualities that are needed by those who want to enter that Kingdom, especially the Eight Beatitudes. They must be persons who (1) are poor in spirit, (2) mourn for others, (3) possess true meekness, (4) hunger and thirst for justice, (5) show mercy to others, (6) exhibit sincerity of heart, (7) act as true peacemakers, and (8) suffer persecution for Your sake.

Your words in the Beatitudes contain the most important teaching of the Kingdom. Then You followed them up with words encouraging people to follow the whole law of God, to forgive enemies, to do good works for God alone, to lay up treasures in heaven, to bear good fruit, to pray, to trust in God and avoid needless worrying, to refrain from judging others, and to do the Will of Your Father.

One day, while You were preaching a woman from the crowd cried out that Your Mother was blessed for having borne You. You answered, "Rather, blessed are those who hear the Word of God and keep it." You thus indicated that Mary was the most blessed of all because she heard every Word of God and kept it.

Help me to seek forgiveness for my sins and to carry out all the duties of a member of the Kingdom of God—most of all to hear Your Word and keep it.

4th Luminous Mystery

The Transfiguration of Our Lord

JESUS, one day You took Peter, James, and John up a high mountain away from everyone else. Then a change came over You. Your face shone like the sun, and Your clothes became as white as light. On Your face there was a heavenly majesty. And Moses and Elijah came down from heaven to talk with You.

Then a bright cloud covered them with shadow, and from the cloud there came a voice that said, "This is My Son, the Beloved; He enjoys My favor. Listen to Him."

The three disciples fell down and worshiped, because they were overcome with fear. Then You came and touched them and said, "Get up and do not be afraid." When they raised their eyes, You stood there alone with a look of peace and light. You urged them not to tell anyone about what they had seen and heard until You were risen from the dead.

Jesus, in Your Transfiguration You allowed a ray of Your hidden Divine Glory to shine through Your human body, as the sun shines through the clouds that seek to veil it. You merely permitted to be recognized for a few moments something of the brightness of Your glorified Body after Your Resurrection.

Moses and Elijah appeared in order to do homage to You and adore You, for the Law (i.e., Moses) and the Prophets (i.e., Elijah) were Your servants. They came to hear that You would accomplish the redemption of all humankind by Your Passion and Death.

The shining cloud and the loud voice were a solemn confirmation of Your Divinity and Your office as Prophet and Priest, for the appearance of a bright cloud was the sign of the presence of God. As at Your Baptism by John in the Jordan, so now Your Father gloriously bore witness to His Son.

Jesus, help me to carry out what Your Father commanded the Apostles to do—i.e., listen to You and experience Your Passion and Resurrection and be transfigured by the Holy Spirit. Enable me to become a new Person in You.

5th Luminous Mystery

Christ's Institution of the Eucharist

 JESUS, as You were partaking of the Last Supper with Your disciples, You took some bread and said the blessing. You broke it and gave it to the disciples, saying, "Take this and eat. This is My Body."

Then You took a cup, and when You had offered thanks, gave it to them, saying, "Drink from this, for this is My Blood, the Blood of the New Covenant, which is to be poured out for the forgiveness of sins. Do this in memory of Me."

The Last Supper was the solemn opening of Your holy Passion; in it You gave a pledge that on the next day You would suffer Death for the world's salvation. For the first time You pronounced the words of sublime mystery by which You changed bread and wine into Your sacred Body and Blood.

Thus, the Eucharist is a memorial of Your Passion, Death, and Resurrection. The sacrifice of the Cross was offered beforehand in a spiritual manner.

Jesus, You thus bequeathed to the Church her greatest treasure and chief riches—the Blessed Sacrament. It is her very heart.

I believe that the Holy Eucharist is the greatest of the Sacraments because You, the Divine Redeemer of the world, give me Your Body and Blood, Soul and Divinity under the appearances of bread and wine.

In giving Yourself, You bestow upon me the highest pledge of salvation and the best means of attaining it. You nourish my soul with Your own life and unite it with God. Let me give You the best proof that I am grateful to You—by participating at each Eucharist fully, consciously, and actively and by receiving You frequently and devoutly so that I may save my soul.

THIRD AND SEVENTH DAY
1st Sorrowful Mystery
The Agony in the Garden

JESUS, the time has come for Your holy Passion to begin. You already feel the burden of suffering weigh heavily upon You in the Garden of Olives.

Yours is the suffering of the soul. Fear takes hold of You—fear caused by the certainty and nearness of Your Death and the sufferings that are to bring it about. You experience disgust at the thought of the sins for which You are to suffer so much. How terrible are these sins of all races and ages in all their vileness and malice as compared with God's supreme authority, infinite goodness, justice, and beauty!

Sadness fills the very depths of Your soul, sadness caused by the knowledge of the small result You will gain by all Your sacrifices, how people will neglect Your Church, or misuse it to their own ruin. All these dreadful pictures rise before You and cut You to the very Heart. You are sorrowful unto death.

You pray: "Father, if it is Your Will, take this cup from Me; yet not My will but Yours be done." Your sweat becomes like drops of blood falling to the ground.

Help me to show my gratitude for Your generosity by true contrition for my sins and by a sincere love for You, my best Friend and my God.

2nd Sorrowful Mystery

The Scourging at the Pillar

JESUS, Pilate sentences You to be beaten into a pitiable condition in order to arouse the compassion of the Jews. You are to endure the dreadful suffering of a Roman scourging, cruel enough to be reserved only for murderers and slaves— and You are the Son of God!

Your virginal flesh is unveiled in the sight of harsh and inhuman soldiers. After Your wrists have been bound with cords and Your Body drawn up so that Your face is turned to the pillar, they begin their blood work. The strokes of the scourges fall with terrible force upon Your bare back and shoulders. Your body trembles with pain beneath the mighty blows, unlimited in number and severity, that burn like fire upon Your skin and cause it to break and swell.

Your Precious Blood oozes forth and trickles down in little streams to the dirty floor. Pain pierces its way to Your very soul, and forces tears from Your eyes and moans from Your lips.

Love makes You endure the scourge of suffering to prevent the scourge of God's just wrath from falling upon me to atone for my sins of impurity. I thank You for this love, and I beg You to help me love You in return and turn away from every sin.

3rd Sorrowful Mystery

The Crowning with Thorns

JESUS, the soldiers make You a mock-king. They tear the clothes from Your bleeding shoulders and cover You with a soldier's cast-off cloak to serve as Your royal robe. They make You sit down upon the broken base of a pillar as upon a throne. Above Your tearful eyes they set a crown of sharp thorns and brutally force it down into Your scalp and entangle it in Your hair. This crown of shame is man's highest contempt for Your Divine Kingship.

As a scepter they put into Your right hand a reed. You sit there, bowed with pain, the picture of complete wretchedness, and yet You are the living God Who at this moment wield a scepter of might over innumerable Angel-hosts. You are the Messiah, the Long-Expected of the nations, and yet You are mocked as a fool. You are the Creator of the universe and all the living, and yet Your creatures give You a crown of shame.

I now bend my knee before You, and pledge unending loyalty to You, my Divine King. Once I bent the knee in contempt of You and Your holy commandments; now I bend it in sincerest love and adoration.

4th Sorrowful Mystery

The Carrying of the Cross

JESUS, You and the Cross are at last together, and Your Heart is already nailed to it. How tenderly You fix Your gaze upon it, press it to Your Heart, and lovingly kiss it. Although You receive the Cross from the kindly hand of Your Father in heaven, it is really I who place its heavy load upon Your bruised shoulder.

The Cross is the symbol of Your tenderest love, the altar on which You are to be sacrificed as the Lamb of God Who takes away the sins of the world. The Cross is the instrument of Your mercy, the trophy of Your victory, and yet You must now feel the disgrace of it as You begin Your last journey for love of me.

I can never understand the depth of suffering to which You consent in receiving Your Cross. Your whole being is crushed by the weight of my sins. You have taught me that Your command to follow You to Calvary is a condition of everlasting happiness. Teach me to bear my pains and disappointments patiently in atonement for my sins. Make my cross of life Your own, and help me to love my sufferings as You love Your Cross.

5th Sorrowful Mystery

The Crucifixion

JESUS, at last Calvary is reached. The soldiers seize You roughly and strip the garments from Your torn body. I see how the wounds inflicted by the scourges are again torn open when You are stripped of Your garments. Strip me of all sinfulness and clothe my poor soul with Your own purity and holiness.

Into each of Your hands and then into Your feet the executioners hammer a heavy nail. Now You lie fastened upon Your hard bed, Your deathbed, with Your head resting upon the painful pillow of Your crown of thorns. Your glances are directed upward to Your Father in entire resignation to His Divine Will, as you pray, "Father forgive them, for they do not know what they are doing." Pray to the Father to forgive me, for my sins nailed You to the Cross, but I, too, did not know what I was doing.

Strong arms lift You aloft and You are left hanging there between heaven and earth, like a criminal, to die slowly amid the terrible torture of body and bitter sadness of soul.

Your fading eyes gaze into the darkened heavens as You cry out with a loud voice, "Father, into Your hands I commend My spirit." Then You bend Your thorn-crowned head in submission to the Will of Your Father and to death. You have died that I might live.

I thank You for Your love for me. May I always live for love of You.

FOURTH, EIGHTH, AND NINTH DAY

1st Glorious Mystery

The Resurrection

JESUS, after Your burial Your enemies sealed the opening of Your tomb and set the guards; they went their way rejoicing that they had conquered You at last. But, by Your own Divine power You rise, as You promised, a glorious Victor.

The earth quakes as You come forth from the tomb, and the guards tremble with fear. Your body now shines like the sun. The wounds of Your hands and feet sparkle like precious jewels. Death is conquered, its victory broken, its sting destroyed. You triumph not for Yourself alone, but that I too may triumph over the grave.

May this Mystery strengthen my hope in another and a better life after death, the resurrection of my body on the last day, and an eternity of happiness. I firmly hope that You will keep Your promise to me and raise me up glorified. Through Your glorious Resurrection I hope that You will make my body like Your own in glory and life, and permit me to dwell with You in heaven.

2nd Glorious Mystery
The Ascension

JESUS, on the fortieth day after Your Resurrection, after having trained Your Apostles for their high calling to establish the Kingdom of God on earth, You go with them to the Mount of Olives. Standing on the summit of that same mountain which had been the scene of the beginning of Your Passion, and streaming with light as at the moment of Your Transfiguration, You prepare to ascend on high to where the glories of heaven await You.

You bless Your loving Mother and Your Apostles and disciples and bid them farewell. A cloud receives You out of their sight. How deep is their sorrow at parting from You! How keen their longing to follow You!

The countless blessed spirits whom You have released from limbo accompany You as the first fruits of the Redemption. All the hosts of heaven's Angels come out to meet You, the Savior of the world. As You take Your place beside Your heavenly Father, the whole court of heaven gives forth a glorious song of praise. I rejoice with You in this perfect attainment of Your glory. When the struggle of this life is over, give me the grace to share Your joy and triumph in heaven for all eternity.

3rd Glorious Mystery

The Descent of the Holy Spirit

JESUS, I thank You for fulfilling Your gracious promise: "I will ask the Father and He will give You another Paraclete, to be with You always."

Holy Spirit, on the fiftieth day after the Resurrection of Jesus, in the midst of a mighty wind, You descend upon the Blessed Virgin, the Apostles and disciples in the Upper Room.

You appear under the form of tongues of fire, because you fill the Apostles with truth and prepare them to bear witness to Jesus. You pour forth in them Your love ardent as a flame, powerful as a violent wind, for You are the personal Love of the Father and the Son in the life of God.

Being filled with Your Divine grace, they go forth fearlessly to preach Jesus Christ with great power and success. You come upon the Infant Church to give it Divine life, to enlighten and preserve it from error and to make it perfect in holiness.

You are, in the Church, what the soul is to the body: the spirit that animates it and protects its unity. Your Divine action produces marvels of grace in the souls of people. Glorify Jesus by spreading His Church throughout the world.

May Your gift of grace enable me one day to gaze upon the sight of God in all His beauty, and to enjoy without end the sweetness and bliss of Your Divine love!

4th Glorious Mystery

The Assumption of Mary

MARY, you obey the law of death, but your death is rather a peaceful slumber, a gentle separation of the soul from the body. Your soul reaches such a degree of love that it seems unable to rest any longer except in the blissful love of the Blessed Trinity.

Your soul sweetly speeds to enjoy the blessed vision of God, and leaves your immaculate body silent and motionless, though very beautiful, in the sleep of death. But soon your fair soul is again united to your body which lies peacefully in the tomb, and suddenly you stand immortal and glorified, clothed in queenly glory. As the Angels sing their hymns of praise, you are raised on high to the Kingdom of glory by God's own power.

There the heavenly citizens bow their heads in humble reverence before you. Who can tell the sweetness of that loving embrace whereby Jesus welcomes and admits you, His own Virgin

Mother, to unending union with Him in the glory of heaven.

Your peaceful tomb has been reopened by the Apostles and found to be empty. Beautiful flowers fill the place where your body has lain, and heavenly music is heard about your empty tomb. The Apostles now realize that you have been taken up into heaven, soul and body.

Help me in my life's true work: to choose virtue and reject sin. Protect me from the danger of temptation, and lead me in the path of virtue till the day of my judgment, that I may share your glory forever.

5th Glorious Mystery

Crowning of Mary in Heaven

MARY, in spirit I behold how Jesus leads you to a throne of glory in heaven next to His own. As you tasted the bitterness of pain and sorrow with Him on earth, you will now enjoy the sweetness of eternal bliss with Him in heaven. You have worn a crown of thorns with Jesus; you will now wear a crown of gold and precious stones even as He does.

I rejoice with you as I see Him put this most beautiful crown upon your head, while all the Angels and Saints acclaim you as their Queen.

Your immaculate Heart beats in unison with the Divine Heart of Jesus, which is now shedding upon you with great delight the love of God made Man. You bow to the Most Blessed Trinity in deepest humility and again utter your prayer of praise: "My being proclaims the greatness of the Lord, my spirit finds joy in God my savior, for God Who is mighty has done great things for me, holy is His Name." You then turn with joy to the Angels and Saints and graciously accept their homage.

May the glorious beauty of your crowning in heaven fill my heart with an ardent longing for the joys of heaven. Through your intercession and tender mercy may I reach the glorious Kingdom of Heaven, there to be happy with Jesus and you for all eternity!

Prayer

℣. Pray for us, O holy Mother of God.

℟. *That we may be made worthy of the promises of Christ.*

LET us pray. God, Whose only-begotten Son by His Life, Death, and Resurrection obtained for us the rewards of eternal salvation grant, we beg of You, that meditating upon these Mysteries in the most Holy Rosary of the Blessed Virgin Mary, we may both imitate what they contain and obtain what they promise. Through Christ our Lord. ℟. *Amen.*